Royal Words
to Guide Your Day:
30 Days
of Devotion
and Transformation

Michele L. Smith

Royal Words to Guide Your Day:
30 Days of Devotion and Transformation

Scripture quotations in this publication are taken from the King James Version unless otherwise noted.

ISBN-13: 978-0-692-52087-1
ISBN-10: 0-692-52087-2

Cover Design and Interior Layout Design by Donna Osborn Clark at www.CreationByDonna.com

Published by Royal Word Publications
All Rights Reserved
Printed in the United States of America

Address inquiries to:
Michele Smith
404 E. 1st Street
Unit 1445
Long Beach, CA 90802

This book is dedicated to: Brenda, Carloyn, Cristine, Katrina, Jacqueline S., Jacqueline T., Trina and Willene. Each of you a flower in my life's bouquet. In your own unique and precious way you all added light to my dark days as I weathered this season's storm.

A basic reality in this life is that we all struggle. We all hurt and have hurt others. There are times we all feel lost. It isn't all we are, but definitely part of who we are. For allowing me to be transparent and accepting me in all my flaws, thank you.

Every woman needs one of each of these friends: Someone who will listen to all your secrets, no matter how ugly and not tell, someone who will share the gallon of ice cream and chocolate molten lava cake in times of stress, someone who will tell you the truth even when it's not what you want to hear, someone who will take off her earrings and go to blows, and someone who will be the clown to make you laugh. I am blessed to have such a circle of women in you. Thank you for being you and for all that you do.

For your presence and your prayers, I am grateful. For your love, I am ever indebted. I love you and appreciate you. I pray that God continue to grow and prosper you in every area of your lives.

Acknowledgments

Aliyah Brielle thank you for the note you gave me that said you were proud of me because I never give up. For such a young princess, there are times you are wise beyond your years. Thank you for being interested in my writing and for allowing me to help you write. Thank you for all the times you make me laugh with your jokes, funny faces and silly songs. Your book is going to be just as amazing as you are. I love you to the heavens and beyond.

Alijah Ivory ever since you were born you have been a blessing to me. Thank you for all the questions you ask, the things you challenge me to think about and the fun videos you make me watch. Thank you for the hugs, kisses, smiles and love you give me every day. I love you to infinity and beyond.

Donna Osborn Clark, thank you doesn't seem nearly sufficient my sister for all you have done for me. Just as in times past, you've been right in my corner, available to me by phone, email day and night, not to mention your prayers! I will ever be grateful to God for the Divine Appointment He made between you and I. Thank you beautiful for all you did to help me bring this one to the fruition. May God continue to anoint your hands, enlarge your territory and bless your labor of love as only He can. You are a gem in my life treasure chest and I value you more than there's room here to write. Hugs and love, always.

Dr. Sanders White, Sr., my pastor, spiritual father and mentor. You continue to keep me in awe of your steadfastness, commitment and unrelenting faith. Thank you for being such an exemplary witness of Christ. Thank you for your prayers, words of encouragement and the lessons you teach me about faith, life and growing in humility. The battle continues and together we shall STAND!

Thank you to everyone that follows me on social media, prays for me, or has sown into my life in word or deed. Thank you for allowing me to pour out of my mind, heart and spirit into your lives. I bless and praise God for each of you. Please know that Who You Are Makes a Difference.

The many tasks we face each day can burden and oppress, but spending time with God each day can bring relief from stress.

The Knots Prayer

Dear God:
Please untie the knots
That are in my mind,
My heart and my life.
Remove the have nots,
The can nots and the do nots
That I have in my mind.
Erase the will nots,
May nots, and might nots
That may find a home
In my heart.
Release me from the could nots,
Would nots, and should nots
That obstruct my life.
And most of all.
Dear God,
I ask that you remove from my mind,
My heart, and my life
All of the 'am nots'
That I have allowed to hold me back,
Especially the thought
That I am not good enough.
Amen

Author Known to God

B egin your day with…

L ove in your heart…

E xpect blessings…

S hare goodness

S hine bright like a diamond

I nspire someone

N ever forget that

G od is with you all the time

S o expect God's best always

Introduction

Welcome to 30 Days of Devotion and Transformation. The goal of this book is to provoke you to think, prompt you to act, encourage you to change and empower you to grow.

Each day there is a passage of scripture and a topic, accompanied by a section for you to record your personal reflections and prayers. At the end of each week you can record your blessings and gratitude.

There is a Bible Reading Plan located at the back of the book. You can start it at any time. Following the daily plan, you will read the entire Bible through in one year.

If you don't know the purpose of a thing, you will abuse it. The Bible says wisdom is the principle thing and in all your getting, get an understanding. Following are the definitions of devotion and transformation to facilitate your understanding of what you are doing and what you should accomplish as you journey through Royal Words to Guide Your Day.

Be encouraged as you embark on your path of devotion and transformation.

Love and blessings.

Devotion
de•vo•tion
[di'vōSHən]

NOUN
love, loyalty, or enthusiasm for a person, activity, or cause:
synonyms: loyalty • faithfulness • fidelity • constancy
• commitment •
*religious worship or observance:
"the order's aim was to live a life of devotion"

synonyms: devoutness • piety • religiousness • spirituality
• holiness • sanctity
*prayers or religious observances.
synonyms: religious worship • worship • religious observance
• prayers

Transformation
trans•for•ma•tion
[transfər'māSHən]

NOUN
a thorough or dramatic change in form or appearance:
"its landscape has undergone a radical transformation"

synonyms: change • alteration • conversion • metamorphosis
• overhaul • reshaping • reconstruction • rebuilding
• rearrangement • reworking • renewal • revamp • remake •

Table of Contents

Day 1 - Liberty for All

This Day in History: The Emancipation Proclamation takes effect, January 1, 1863.

Today's Verse: *And ye shall know the truth, and the truth shall make you free.* **John 8:32**

Once upon a time, there was a colorless tiger. All his shades were greys, blacks and whites. His lack of color made him so famous that the world's greatest painters had come to his zoo to try to put some color on him. None of the succeeded, as the colors would always just drip off his skin.

Then along came Can Cough the crazy painter. He was a strange guy who traveled all about, happily painting with his brush. Well, it would be more accurate to say that he moved his brush about, as if to paint; because he never put any paint on his brush, and neither did he use canvas or paper. He painted the air, and that's why they called him Van Cough. So, when he said he wanted to paint the colorless tiger, everyone had a good laugh.

When entering the tiger's cage he began whispering in the animal's ear, and moving his dry brush up and down the tiger's body. And to everyone's surprise, the tiger's skin started to take on color, and these were the most vivid colors any tiger had ever had. Van Cough spent a long time whispering to the animal, and making slight adjustments to his painting. The result was truly beautiful.

Inquiring minds wanted to know the painter's secret. He advised that his brush was only good for painting real life, and that to do so he didn't need colors. He painted the tiger using a phrase he repeatedly whispered in his ear: "In just a few days you will be free again, you shall see."

And seeing how sad the tiger had been in his captivity, and how joyful the tiger now seemed at the prospect of freedom, the zoo authorities took him to the forest and set him free, where he would never again lose his color.

Throughout this earthly life, there are times when you will feel trapped like the colorless tiger. Situations, circumstances, failed relationships, financial worries, health concerns all can have one in a state of sadness and loneliness. Having no control can be daunting. Be encouraged in the knowledge that you too have a Van Cough painter angel. One who will hold you close and whisper in your ear. One who will restore your vibrancy, your joy, your hope. His name is Jesus. Over 2,000 years ago Jesus died on the cross at Calvary to secure your freedom. He gave His life for all humanity to have liberty. Freedom is yours for the taking. Although there may be times that it seems you are boxed in, the Holy Spirit is only a prayer away. You don't ever have to accept the cage others may try to fit you in. You have Liberty in Christ Jesus. Bask in the beauty of your Freedom and Live Your Life Royally.

Today's Reflection:

Today's Prayer:

Day 2 - Empty Vessels

This Day in History: Theodor Geisel, better known to the world as Dr. Seuss, the author and illustrator of such beloved children's books as "The Cat in the Hat" and "Green Eggs and Ham," is born in Springfield, Massachusetts, March 2, 1904.

Today's Verse: *And unto one he gave five talents, to another two, and to another one; to every man according to his several ability; and straightway took his journey. Then he that had received the five talents went and traded with the same, and made them other five talents. And likewise he that had received two, he also gained other two. But he that had received one went and digged in the earth, and hid his lord's money. After a long time the lord of those servants cometh, and reckoneth with them. Then he which had received the one talent came and said, Lord, I knew thee that thou art an hard man, reaping where thou hast not sown, and gathering where thou hast not strawed: And I was afraid, and went and hid thy talent in the earth: lo, there thou hast that is thine.* **Matthew 25:15-19, 24-25 (Read vs14-25)**

In this passage we learn of the men that Jesus entrusted a number of talents. When it came time for them to report what they had done with that which they were entrusted, it is discovered that one of the men buried his talent. In so doing he wasted time, and delayed the potential return on investment of the talent. God has entrusted each of us with talents as well that we will be held accountable for. When we greet the Master face to face, He will ask what we did with that He gave us. You are the manager of your gifts: your personality, your abilities, and your heart. *"Each of you should use whatever gift he has received to serve others, faithfully administering God's grace in its various forms"* (1 Peter 4:10 NIV). If you had to stand before the Lord today, what would your report say? Your gifts and talents are like muscles. As you use them, they will grow. Pour out of yourself into the lives of others so you can stand before God an empty vessel. God's benefit package is better than anything corporate America could ever give you. Pour out today and Receive His Royal blessings.

Michele L. Smith

Today's Reflection:

Today's Prayer:

6

Day 3 - A Beautiful Mind

Today's Verse: I beseech you therefore, brethren, by the mercies of God, that ye present your bodies a living sacrifice, holy, acceptable unto God, which is your reasonable service. And be ye not conformed to this world: but be ye transformed by the renewing of your mind that ye may prove what is that good, and acceptable, and perfect, will of God. **Romans 12:1-2**

You think 60,000 thoughts each day. Don't waste 59,999 of them on negative thinking. A negative mind will never give you a positive life.

Renewing your mind and changing your thoughts is an ongoing process. One that must be worked each day. Just as you bathe yourself and brush your teeth, so must the routine of renewing your mind become ingrained in your daily activities. You must be willing to put forth the effort to believe that you are a beautiful soul. Who you are makes a difference. You've got the power to change situations, circumstances: to make a difference in your life and the lives of others. Without you, someone else's life puzzle is missing a piece. Believe in the power you possess through the grace of our Lord Jesus. Allow your power and beauty to permeate the atmosphere. Step out in faith. No one else can believe for you. You have to know in your beautiful mind that no one else can do what you do the way you do it. Challenge yourself to renew your mind each day. Be your best you and Live Your Life Royally.

Today's Reflection:

Today's Prayer:

Day 4 - A New Thing

Today's Verse: *Remember ye not the former things, neither consider the things of old. Behold, I will do a new thing; now it shall spring forth; shall ye not know it? I will even make a way in the wilderness, and rivers in the desert. The beast of the field shall honour me, the dragons and the owls: because I give waters in the wilderness, and rivers in the desert, to give drink to my people, my chosen.* **Isaiah 43:18-20**

It's been almost twelve years (at press time), since Mark Zuckerberg followed his heart, implemented his vision and forever changed how we communicate and interact with friends, family and people all around the world. Technology continues to advance, taking us to new and amazing heights in social, familial and professional arenas.

Just as technology continues to evolve, so should our walk with the Lord. God is ever present and always waiting to release a new thing in your life. Whether it be a new relationship, new job, business, ministry or hobby there is never a shortage of blessings available to you. Your bank account today may not contain sufficient funds to launch that multi-million dollar corporation, but God's bank is still in the funding business. You may not have the qualifications for that promotion on your job, but God is doling out Favor. Sometimes we have not because we ask not. Sometimes we are operating in the definition of insanity: doing the same thing, the same way over and over expecting a different result.

Today you have a clean slate. A fresh opportunity to do a new thing. Sometimes you have to step into new places to get your new. Step out in faith today, visit a new place, taste a food you've never eaten, make a new friend. Let Go and Let God do a New Thing in your life today.

Michele L. Smith

Today's Reflection:

Today's Prayer:

Day 5 - Fly Like an Eagle

Today's Verse: *But those who wait upon the Lord [who expect, look for, and hope in Him] shall change and renew their strength and power, they shall lift their wings and mount up [close to God] as eagles [mount up to the sun]; they shall run and not be weary, they shall walk and not faint to become tired.* **Isaiah 40:31**

Did you know that an eagle knows when a storm is coming? In fact, it knows long before the storm approaches. The eagle flies to a high spot and waits for the winds to come. While the storm rages below, the eagle is above it. An eagle does not try to escape the storm but uses it to lift itself higher.

When the storms of life come upon us, like the eagle, we can fly above them and ride the winds of the storm that bring disappointment, trial, sickness, failure and chaos into our lives. Our past is part of our purpose, God does not intend for us to dwell there. He does not want you to settle for what happened in the storm of your yesterday. You cannot change the tragedies of your childhood, the pitfalls of past relationships or the drama in last week's storm. You can make the necessary adjustments to move forward in positive progress. God is calling you to SOAR today. God has something special in store for your today. In order to obtain it, you must be willing to fly like an eagle. Don't be so caught up in looking back, that you forget to look up. This will cause you to crash mid-air. It may feel as though God has forgotten you. Like you are all alone in the journey. Eagles fly solo. When you allow God to be your life pilot, you are never alone. His time is not our time. He is always on time. He has an amazing flight plan for you. Are you ready? Will you fly with the best pilot ever known to man? Will you open your mind, heart and spirit to SOAR like the eagle He created you to be? Your plane is at the loading gate...Prepare for take-off.

Today's Reflection:

Today's Prayer:

Blessings and Gratitude

Of whom the whole family in heaven and earth is named, That he would grant you, according to the riches of his glory, to be strengthened with might by his Spirit in the inner man; That Christ may dwell in your hearts by faith; that ye, being rooted and grounded in love, May be able to comprehend with all saints what is the breadth, and length, and depth, and height; And to know the love of Christ, which passeth knowledge, that ye might be filled with all the fullness of God. **Ephesians 3:15-19**

"Progress is impossible without change, and those who cannot change their minds cannot change anything." George Bernard Shaw

Day 6 - How Does Your Garden Grow?

This Day in History: Jerry Lewis' 28th Muscular Dystrophy telethon raises $46,014,922.00, September 6, 1993.

Today's Verse: They will be like a tree planted by the water that sends out its roots by the stream. It does not fear when heat comes; its leaves are always green. It has no worries in a year of drought and never fails to bear fruit. **Jeremiah 17:8 (NIV)**

Reaping and Sowing is a biblical principle. Often we quote it for our benefit or to lay blame on others: *"You gonna reap what you sow."* Typically this is done when we disagree with someone or believe they have wronged us in some way. Actually, we need not concern ourselves with the next person's harvest. Their seeds will produce blossoms or weeds just as our own. Our focus should be on what kind of seeds we are planting and what our harvest will bring. Sowing in peace results in peace. Sowing service guarantees that you will be served in return. Planting a monetary seed sets the release of financial blessings to come to you. Likewise, planting seeds of negativity will have the same outcome. Sowing discord brings confusion. Sowing anger reaps anger and so on. What kinds of seeds are you planting in your life garden? God has planted you on good soil. Plant seeds that will produce sweet fruits of the spirit, releasing the harvest of God's abundant blessings in your life.

Today's Reflection:

Today's Prayer:

Day 7 - Trust in the Lord

This Day in History: Pope Paul VI & Orthodox Patriarch Athenagoras I simultaneously lift mutual excommunications that led to split of 2 churches in 1054, December 7, 1965.

Today's Verse: *Those who trust in the LORD are as secure as Mount Zion; they will not be defeated but will endure forever. Just as the mountains surround Jerusalem, so the Lord surrounds his people, both now and forever.* **Psalm 125:1-2 (NLT)**

The airwaves were all abuzz on the evening of June 17, 2015, following a mass shooting at Emanuel African Methodist Episcopal Church in downtown Charleston, South Carolina. During a prayer service, nine people were killed by a gunman: Cynthia Hurd; Susie Jackson; Ethel Lee Lance, Depayne Middleton; Reverend Clementa C. Pinckney; Tywanza Sanders; Reverend Daniel Simmons and Reverend Sharonda Coleman-Singleton. The morning after the attack, police arrested a suspect, identified some time later as 21-year old Dylann Roof. Roof was arrested in Shelby, North Carolina. He later confessed hoping to incite a race war as his motive for the shooting.

Our hearts and spirits grieve for all affected. What should be noted here is that each of the nine individuals who died were exactly where they were supposed be, doing exactly what they knew best – praying and studying the Word of God. Sharing a time of fellowship with a stranger among them. Each of them died living their Trust in the Lord. For their faith, they were persecuted just as Jesus was. The media makes money on ratings sensationalizing incidents like these. Some will use opportunities as this to act out their own anger or irrational thought processes. It is crucial that we understand that no matter what is going on in the world around us, we must Trust God. Trust God and Pray. War in the spirit on behalf of those like Dylann Roof who do have clarity of mind to do so for themselves. Those who trust in the LORD are as secure as Mount Zion; they will not be defeated but endure forever. Let us not allow the nine lives taken deter our faith. Trust in the Lord and Live Your Life Royally.

Michele L. Smith

Today's Reflection:

Today's Prayer:

A Grain of Faith

I am mustard seed, small I am, small indeed,
Created He me and named me mustard seed.
I am praying for you, interceding daily,
That you can begin with me to trust and believe.
That you learn to understand me,
The mustard seed.
Because I have no limbs to walk,
Nor eyes to see,
And when planted,
I will not become the tallest tree.
Yet I represent all that God asks of you,
To have faith and believe that He is real and true.
When you look at me what do you see?
I pray you see the reflection of the Father's beauty,
Yes, in something as small and insignificant as me.
God abounds powerful and oh so mighty,
If you can manage to muster faith as large as me.
Nothing is impossible,
Blessings will flow bountifully.
Faith is the foundation of life and salvation,
Without faith life is hopeless and full of destruction.
Keep me close, keep His word near,
Pray your prayers in faith,
And God will always hear.
The life that you are seeking begins here with me,
Faith as a grain of mustard seed.
Everything that seek will surely be yours
When you let go and let God
When you...Truly BELIEVE!

Day 8 - Promises Matter

Today's Verse: *And God said, This is the token of the covenant which I make between me and you and every living creature that is with you, for perpetual generations: I do set my bow in the cloud, and it shall be for a token of a covenant between me and the earth.* **Genesis 9:12-13**

God made a covenant (promise) in the ninth Chapter of Genesis between himself and the earth. The Bible also tells us in Numbers 23:19, *God is not a man, that he should lie; neither the son of man, that he should repent: hath he said, and shall he not do it? or hath he spoken, and shall he not make it good?*

Many have said to me, *"promises are made to be broken."* I emphatically disagree. It is better not to promise than to make a promise and break it. If we are honest, we'll admit we have all done it, but as we know better we must strive to do better. When we make a promise, those we commit to believe in us wholeheartedly. Much like in the days of old when contracts were executed on a handshake. People expect us to be true to our word. How many times have you said, *"My word is my bond,"* and turned around to break the very commitment you gave your word to fulfill? Once we break a promise, our trust level is diminished. If the pattern continues, it can be shattered completely. Begin to make it a practice to pray before you promise. It's okay to say, *"I'll pray on it and follow up with you soon."* God is looking for men and women of character and integrity. For those who will fulfill their commitments. To walk in His truth and not be a stumbling block to others through secrets, lies and broken promises. Know that God is not a man that He will lie. Stand on His Promises to Live Your Life Royally.

Michele L. Smith

Today's Reflection:

Today's Prayer:

Day 9 - Balanced Life

Today's Verse: *Give all your worries and cares to God, for he cares about you.* **I Peter 5:7**

Had you met Hannah Loaring in 2010, you would have come face-to-face with a 30-year old, $24,000 in debt and recently brokenhearted. But today she is no longer that down and out person. Loaring is now an award winning blogger, world traveler and co-founder of her own graphic and Web design business, Further Bound. Loaring took on four jobs to pay off the large debt she accumulated in her 20's. She worked often between 80 and 100 hours per week as a waitress, babysitter, shop assistant and freelance designer. She did so for 18 months. When she had earned double the amount she owed in debt, she sold everything she owned, quit all of her jobs and bought a one-way ticket to India. Today, Hanna Loaring lives her dream…a balanced life.

Are you living a balanced life? Are you overwhelmed by all that you are trying to juggle? Maintaining balance is important as you travel your way through this life. When you are unbalanced in any area, the other areas of your life will undoubtedly suffer at some point. *No temptation has overtaken you except what is common to mankind. And God is faithful; he will not let you be tempted beyond what you can bear. But when you are tempted, he will also provide a way out so that you can endure it.* I Corinthians 10:13 (NIV). Take responsibility for what you are piling on your life plate. Do not

Michele L. Smith

shop when you are emotional. Do not make permanent decisions based on temporary feelings. Eat for your health, not for your comfort. If you are angry or frustrated, pray before you lash out. Life is about balance. Be kind, but don't let people abuse you. Be content, but never stop learning. Be part of the solution, don't perpetuate the problem. Never stop improving yourself. Cast your cares upon the Lord for He cares for you.

Today's Reflection:

Today's Prayer:

Day 10 - Are You Being Robbed?

Today's Verse: *Look carefully then how you walk, not as unwise but as wise, making the best use of the time, because the days are evil. Therefore do not be foolish, but understand what the will of the Lord is.* **Ephesians 5:15-17 (ESV)**

Don't worry. We have plenty of time to do our homework, Angie grinned as she headed to the school gates. Besides this 'huge assignment' is due in two weeks. That's plenty of time!

Three days before the assignment is due. WOW. That carnival was so fun, Angie yawned happily after another friend invited her to come to the yearly carnival.

"Hey Angie, have you finished that assignment?" Angie's brain snapped open. The assignment....she hadn't done anything. *'Uhm....N-no.'* Angie replied nervously. Her eyes widened. *"Really? I finished mine two days ago, and the assignment is due in three days. I hope you finish it."* Lizzie quickly waved goodbye to her friend and rushed home.

Angie decided to grab her equipment and do some research. But it was really late so she decided to leave it until tomorrow.

Are you an Angie today? Are you allowing procrastination to rob you? Yes, procrastination is a thief. Procrastination will deceive you into believing you have plenty of time to do that thing and then have you on the verge of a nervous breakdown when at the last minute you haven't even begun. Tomorrow is not promised. All we have is the gift of today. His grace is sufficient for today. Open your grace gift and use it wisely to Live Your Life Royally.

Today's Reflection:

Today's Prayer:

Blessings and Gratitude

Now unto him that is able to do exceeding abundantly above all that we ask or think, according to the power that worketh in us, **Ephesians 3:20**

"Experience is that marvelous thing that enables you to recognize a mistake when you make it again." F.P. Jones

Day 11 - Breaking Point

This Day in History: Harlem, New York voters defy Congress and re-elect Adam Clayton Powell, Jr., April 11, 1967.

Today's Verse: *The LORD will make you the head, not the tail. If you pay attention to the commands of the LORD your God that I give you this day and carefully follow them, you will always be at the top, never at the bottom.* **Deuteronomy 28:13 (NIV)**

James was an auto mechanic whose company started "downsizing," and in the processed he was one of those who were 'let go". He knew he would have to find work elsewhere. It couldn't have come at a worse time, not with the pile of bills, the rising cost of gas (or everything else). Not to mention, caring for his mom who was bed-ridden and living with him, as well as meeting the needs of his wife and children.

Perhaps you have been in a situation like James. It has been said that everyone has a breaking point. That rock bottom place where you can't get any lower. Hitting rock bottom can be debilitating, damaging and devastating. The good news is that you don't have to stay there. You don't have to wallow in a place of hopelessness and despair. You can get up, rise above all you have been or are going through and press forth in purpose. You are precious, valuable and worthy. Don't allow your pride to keep you from grabbing hold of your life line, pulling yourself up and climbing to your destiny. You are destined for greatness. You have the power, gifts and ability to be successful. Dare to Believe in You. Use your rocks to climb. Though you may stumble, stay the course and you will not fall. Don't allow your Breaking Point to be the Point Break of No Return. Rise from the Pit. Push your way to the Palace of Living Your Life Royally.

Today's Reflection:

Today's Prayer:

Day 12 - Secrets and Lies

This Day in History: First United States law requiring medical tests for marriage licenses goes into effect in New York, April 12, 1938.

Today's Verse: *A man's belly shall be satisfied with the fruit of his mouth; and with the increase of his lips shall he be filled. Death and life are in the power of the tongue; and they that love it shall eat the fruit thereof.* **Proverbs 18:20-21**

As one whose childhood and portions of adult life have been shrouded in secrets and lies, I can attest first hand to the pain, devastation and destruction we can cause with our mouths. The old saying, "*sticks and stones may break my bones, but words will never hurt me,*" I believe was intended to discourage us from allowing the power of harsh words to infiltrate our hearts and minds. Sadly, it is a gross misstatement because in truth our words indeed have power. Literally, the power of life and death are in the tongue and it is important to exercise caution in what we allow to roll of this muscle and flow into the atmosphere.

The Bible says in Proverbs 16:16-19 that one of the things the Lord hates is a lying tongue. Further, in John 8:32, He says we will know the truth and the truth will make us free. We can only be Free IF we are willing to accept God's Word as Truth and strive to live His Truth every day.

Things told you in confidence are not to be shared. No matter how strong the urge, do not be tempted into gossip. Knowingly keeping secrets with the intent to harm others is not the will of God. Lying to impress others is unnecessary and unproductive. Omitting or exaggerating the truth to allegedly keep someone from being hurt is deception. A lie straight from the pits of hell and God is not pleased. Yes, the truth may hurt, but it is always better to speak truth. We lie in front of our children and then punish them when they begin to lie. They are only following the example they've been given. Living Truth is an individual choice. You can choose to spin a web of lies and create pits of deception or you can choose to represent and live truth. Study the Word of God. Know the Truth. Speak the Truth. Allow the Truth to Make you FREE and Live Your Life Royally.

Michele L. Smith

Today's Reflection:

Today's Prayer:

Day 13 - Circle of Friends

This Day in History: The trade mark Velcro is registered, May 13, 1958; U.S. Federal Education funding is denied to 12 school districts in the South because of violations of the 1964 Civil Rights Act, May 13, 1966.

Today's Verse: *A man that hath friends must shew himself friendly: and there is a friend that sticketh closer than a brother.* **Proverbs 18:24**

There was a young man who lived by the philosophy that a human has two basic rights in life: to choose his or her life partner and friends, but that the rest are pre-destined such as one can't choose his or her race nor their parents, it's just given. He became distant from his family and chose a circle of friends that once he was out of money and became ill all abandoned him.

Having friends is not bad, but choosing them is very important because one good friend could change your life and one bad friend could ruin your life. While one cannot choose family, God ordained family and we should always love family and remain connected to them. As you move forward in life, there may be seasons in which you need to change your circle of friends. People come into our lives for a reason, a season or a lifetime. Everyone in your circle is not interested in seeing you improve. Press on anyway. Don't allow their lack of vision to put a cloud in your sky. Press on anyway. Don't allow their lack of support distract you from purpose. Press on anyway. Release them when necessary, love them from a distance and Press on anyway. Smiling faces show no traces of the evil that lurks within. Develop a relationship with God and you will always have a friend. Keep God at the Center of your Circle as you Live Your Life Royally.

Michele L. Smith

Today's Reflection:

Today's Prayer:

Day 14 - Flying High

This Day in History: Franklin Deleanor Roosevelt becomes the first president to travel by airplane on U.S. official business, January 14, 1943.

Today's Verse: *But those who wait upon the Lord [who expect, look for, and hope in Him] shall change and renew their strength and power, they shall lift their wings and mount up [close to God] as eagles [mount up to the sun]; they shall run and not be weary, they shall walk and not faint or become tired.* **Isaiah 40:31**

Bree was the first on the plane for a KLM flight from Amsterdam to Johannesburg. She was sitting in window seat 15A. Her plan: to catch a film and a bit of shut-eye before landing. The flight attendant tells her the flight is full. Her heart sinks: there goes my vision of stretching out over two seats. A small boy is sitting in 15C. I wonder who will occupy 15B. A snorer? A talker? Please, no! Then a discussion: the child is standing, bags are moving and the stewardess is orchestrating the move like a seasoned choreographer. In place of the small boy now is a man, a blond Adonis with a ready smile, putting his bags in the overhead locker.

I look up to him and say, *"I think we're going to be lucky..."* These words are prophetic, but at the time I am referring, of course, to the seat between us. The doors shut and 15B remains unoccupied. The plane takes off, and over the empty seat Bree and the blond Adonis strike up the best conversation of her life. By the time they land, plans were being made. *"Do you want to have dinner?"* he asked. *"I do,"* Bree replied. Eight months later she stood facing him, beaming, and say *"I do"* in a garden chapel in Africa.

Bree's patience in the short span of time awaiting departure, allowed her blessing to get in place and assured her marital future. Imagine if she had allowed her thoughts to take over and cause her to act irrationally. Waiting is not always easy, but waiting is often necessary. There is purpose in the waiting. There is preparation in the waiting. There are lessons in the waiting. Whatever you are trusting and believing God for in this season, know that your waiting is not in vain. God has not forgot. Everything that God has promised you shall come to pass in His time. Be Encouraged in the Waiting. Your Best is Yet to Come.

Today's Reflection:

Today's Prayer:

Michele L. Smith

A Mother's Heartache

Twenty three years ago he lay growing in the womb
An anxious mother to be knew that he'd be born soon
Excited and yet nervous about mothering a son
With the first glimpse of his face her heart was won
Joy and happiness grew with him each day
She grew to love him more than she could say
So small and sweet her adorable little boy
For hours she'd sit and watch him play with his toys
The radiance in his smile warmed her heart
A heart burning of a mother's love right from the start
Years passed on and her little boy grew
No longer was he the son his mother thought she knew
Hidden secrets, broken promises, excuses and lies
For the mother and son such became a way of life
Sadness, tears, frustration and pain
All rolled up into a mother's heartache
She questioned, pondered and wondered why
Her son would walk the path of misery and strife
Couldn't he see the mistakes she had made?
Didn't he know life wasn't supposed to be this way?
Bright and intelligent, filled with potential
Why couldn't he see he was destined to be influential?
Why couldn't he see what a difference he could make?
Time passed on and so continued a mother's heartache
She prayed and cried, she moaned and groaned
'Til one day God told her you must leave him alone
He was my son before he was yours
I gave him to you as a gift
I allowed you to care for him
And sometimes you slipped
You've prayed to me and I heard your cry
Yet you keep asking me Why God why?
The reason is that you must leave him with me
Only he and I can work it out so that he is free

Free from the guilt, the hurt and the shame
Free from the pains of feeling betrayed
Free from those things that have him in bondage
Free from the burdens and excess baggage
He is my son and I love him so much
All he needs is to ask for my touch
Until that time you need cry no more
Just trust me like you never have before
Forgive yourself as I have forgiven you
Let me be God and do what I do
The day soon shall come when you will give me praise
For no longer will you suffer a mother's heartache!

Day 15 - Children Are Gifts

This Day in History: Harry Chapin becomes the proud father of his first child, Joshua Burke, in New York City, an event that would eventually inspire him to put his wife's poem, "Cat's In the Cradle," to music, November 15, 1979.

Today's Verse: *Train up a child in the way he should go: and when he is old, he will not depart from it.* **Proverbs 22:6**

A curious child asked his mother: *"Mommy, why some of your hairs turning gray?"*

The mother tried to use this occasion to teach her child: *"It is because of you, dear. Every bad action of yours will turn one of my hairs gray."* The child replied innocently: *"Now I know why grandmother has only gray hairs on her head."*

I imagine many can relate to this parent-child interaction. I admit there have been times that I tried the same tactic. Children are amazing. Their natural boldness often catches us off guard. Their innocence is refreshing and should never be taken from them. Children are precious gifts from God. Parenting is a major responsibility. So much of it is on-the-job training, hit or miss, learn as you go. Each child is fearfully and wonderfully made in the image of God and it is the parent's duty to nurture, encourage, love and discipline them as they grow. God tells us in the above referenced passage to train up a child in the way they should go. This does not mean as we think they should go or how others may want to tell them they should go. This means according to the Word of God and the Will of God for their lives. God's plan for our children is not the same plan he has for us individually. As parents it is important that you pray with your children, teach them how to study God's Word and take them to the house of worship to fellowship with other believers. Encourage your child(ren) to seek God for themselves so that when the time comes and they must make their own choices, they have the wisdom and understanding of how to do so. So that even if they stray away, just as the prodigal's son at some point they will return. Teach your child (ren) that they are precious, valuable and worthy. Teach them that God loves them and it is His Will that they Live Life Royally.

Michele L. Smith

Today's Reflection:

Today's Prayer:

Blessings and Gratitude

Only be thou strong and very courageous, that thou mayest observe to do according to all the law, which Moses my servant commanded thee: turn not from it to the right hand or to the left, that thou mayest prosper withersoever thou goest. **Joshua 1:7**

Michele L. Smith

"The truth is the same from any angle" Unknown

Day 16 - Limitless

This Day in History: Walt Disney launches Epcot Center: Experimental Prototype Community of Tomorrow, November 16, 1965.

Today's Verse: *I returned, and saw under the sun, that the race is not to the swift, nor the battle to the strong, neither yet bread to the wise, nor yet riches to men of understanding, nor yet favour to me of skill, but time and chance happeneth to them all.* **Ecclesiastes 9:11**

Olympic gold medalist Florence "Flo-Jo" Joyner brought style to track and field with form-fitting bodysuits, six-inch fingernails and amazing speed. She epitomized a limitless mindset. Joyner made her Olympic debut in 1984, at the Summer Olympic Games in Los Angeles. There, she won a silver medal for the 200-meter run. She would go on to compete at the national level for more than a decade. Nearly six years after the Seoul Olympics, in 1995, Joyner was honored with an induction into the Track and Field Hall of Fame. She still holds the world records in the 100- and 200-meter events.

Limitations live only in our minds. But if we use our imaginations, our possibilities become limitless. Each of us is uniquely created with imagination and limitless potential. Each day brings new opportunities for us to Become, Create, and Grow. You have the power to overcome obstacles that come your way. Some days you may have to plug along at a jogger's pace. Sometimes you may have to jump the high hurdles. Some days you may have to sprint and others you may have to go the distance pressing against the wind. Preparation for the race

Michele L. Smith

involves mind and body. Do not let your mind become the devil's workshop. Do not allow people or circumstances to limit you. Don't get stuck in the starting block. Keep Dreaming. Keep Believing. Embrace your uniqueness and Live Your Life Limitless.

Today's Reflection:

Today's Prayer:

Day 17 - Life Bouquet

This Day in History: U.S. Congress authorizes paper money, July 17, 1861.

Today's Verse: *There is a time for everything, and a season for every activity under the heavens,* **Ecclesiastes 3:1 (NIV)**

Recently I was having a conversation with a sister friend of mine who was contemplating some decisions regarding a relationship. She was struggling with how she had handled some things in the past and was adamant that no matter what, she had to be true to God and herself. I understood her position and as her friend I wanted her to allow herself to be happy because she deserves it. We all do.

As we talked, God began to show me a bouquet of flowers: Life, love and relationships are likened unto a bouquet of flowers. Initially, some buds are in full bloom, some are still closed. As the connection develops, the petals unfold until such time as the whole bouquet is in full bloom. Time marches on, life happens and change takes place. Petals begin to wilt (relationships wither). Eventually your life flowers die – physically or emotionally. You may press some petals in your memory book, or just empty the vase. You don't say to the flowers: *"Why did you die?"* or *"I'm devastated because you left me,"* because you know it's the natural progression of the flower's life cycle. You simply say goodbye to the flowers and release them. Consider making this practical application to your life: Enjoy the Beauty of it as it is while it is and when it's gone Be Thankful that you had it while it was what it was rather than being angry or hurt that it is no more. Live like there's no tomorrow. Laugh every day. Love like you've never been hurt. Appreciate each flower in your life's bouquet for the love, joy and beauty they add to your existence. Bask in the Beauty of your Life's Bouquet.

Michele L. Smith

Today's Reflection:

Today's Prayer:

Day 18 - Almighty Defender

This Day in History: Susan B. Anthony fined $100 for voting for President, June 18, 1873.

Today's Verse: *For he shall give his angels charge over thee, to keep thee in all thy ways.* **Psalm 91:11**

During the Mau Mau uprising in Kenya in 1960, missionaries Matt and Lora Higgens were returning one night to Nairobi through the heart of Mau Mau territory, where Kenyans and missionaries alike had been killed and dismembered. Seventeen miles outside of Nairobi their Land Rover stopped. Higgens tried to repair the car in the dark, but could not restart it. They spent the night in the car, but claimed Psalm 4:8: *"I will lie down and sleep in peace, for you alone, O Lord, make me dwell in safety."* In the morning they were able to repair the car.

A few weeks later the Higgenses returned to America on furlough. They reported that the night before they left Nairobi, a local pastor had visited them. He told how a member of the Mau Mau had confessed that he and three others had crept up to the car to kill the Higgenses, but when they saw the sixteen men surrounding the car, the Mau Mau left in fear. *"Sixteen men?"* Higgens responded. *"I don't know what you mean!"*

While they were on furlough, a friend Clay Brent asked the Higgenses if they had been in any danger recently. Higgens asked, "Why?" Then Clay said that God had placed a heavy prayer burden on his heart. He called the men of the church, and sixteen of them met together and prayed until the burden lifted. Did God send sixteen angels to represent those men and enforce their prayers? I believe He did. He will never leave you nor forsake you. God will always protect you and when necessary provide a way of escape. God is our Almighty Defender.

Today's Reflection:

Today's Prayer:

Day 19 - Treasure Chest

This Day in History: NY Herald reports gold discovery in California, August 19, 1849.

Today's Verse: *For where your treasure is, there will your heart be also.* **Matthew 6:21**

There lived a farmer in the village. He had five sons. They were all idlers and never helped their father. The father was sad and worried. He tried with all his might to correct them, all in vain. One he got sick and called all his sons together. When they arrived, he asked them to sit and listen very carefully to him. The father said, "My dear sons, I am weak and ill. I may die any moment. There is a lot of money hidden in our fields but I have forgotten where I buried it. Dig up that treasure after my death." Two days later the father died. The sons dug every inch of the tend but found nothing. Since the field was so well ploughed an old man encouraged the sons to sow wheat. The sons sowed the wheat and had a good crop. From the sale of the wheat they earned a lot of money. Then they understood what their father meant. It was really the hidden treasure. From then on the sons worked hard and lived a good life.

What are you tending? Do you know how to locate your hidden treasure? Just as the farmer's sons, God has given you a treasure chest. It is filled with precious nuggets, valuable insights, supernatural strength, whole health, wisdom, wealth, success, joy and prosperity. It is up to you to plough, to dig up your Faith: put your treasures into play and live your best life. People only do what you allow them to. They can only take from your treasure chest if you give them the key. Utilize your inner gems to step up and walk into your purpose, calling and destiny. Open your Treasure Chest…Live Your Life Royally.

Today's Reflection:

Today's Prayer:

Day 20 - Laughter is Good Medicine

Today's Verse: *A merry heart doeth good like medicine: but a broken spirit drieth the bones.* **Proverbs 17:22**

Reginald was terribly overweight, so his doctor placed him on a strict diet. *'I want you to eat regularly for two days, then skip a day, and repeat this procedure for two weeks. The next time I see you, you'll have lost at least five pounds,'* his doctor assured him.

When Reginald returned he shocked his doctor by having lost almost twenty pounds. *'Why, that's amazing,'* the doctor said, greatly impressed, *'You certainly must have followed my instructions.'*

Reginald nodded, *'I'll tell you what though, I thought I was going to drop dead on the third day.'*

'Why, from hunger?' asked his doctor.

'No, from all that skipping.'

Some of the hardest laughs I've ever experienced have come from my grandkids sharing the corniest knock-knock jokes or short stories like Reginald's. It has been scientifically studied and proven that people who laugh on a regular basis, have a positive mindset and live longer than those who don't. The fact that God chose to make mention of laughter in His Word means that it's significant. What makes you laugh? What tickles your fancy? When was the last time you laughed until your jaws hurt? God intended for you to have fun and enjoy this life. He has a sense of humor. Be brave. Take risks. Be sure that a smile is part of your wardrobe every day. Live, Love and Laugh.

Today's Reflection:

Today's Prayer:

Blessings and Gratitude

No weapon that is formed against thee shall prosper; and every tongue that shall rise against thee in judgment thou shalt condemn. This is the heritage of the servants of the LORD, and their righteousness is of me, saith the LORD. **Isaiah 54:17**

Michele L. Smith

*"Never believe that a few caring people can't change the world. For,
indeed, that's all who ever have."* Margaret Mead

Day 21 - Breaking Barriers

This Day in History: Pink Floyds' "Wall" is performed where Berlin Wall once stood, July 21, 1990.

Today's Verse: *By faith the walls of Jericho fell down, after they were compassed about seven days.* **Hebrews 11:30**

All great achievements require effort, persistence and time. It is in the persevering that breakthrough comes. These troubles and sufferings of ours are, after all, quite small and won't last very long. Yet this short time of distress will result in God's richest blessing upon us forever and ever. 2 Corinthians 4:17

A great many people believing the adage: "If you don't succeed, try something else?" end up falling or failing. Success doesn't always come easy. It took Johannes Brahms seven years to finish his famous lullaby. It has jokingly been said that it took so long because he kept falling asleep at the piano. Whatever the reason, he persisted. He didn't give up. He gave time and only God knows how many hundreds of thousands of times his song has been sung or played. The root word of success means to follow through. Holding on in spite of everything, is the winner's quality. 90% of failures result from people giving up too soon.

You are just on the other side of your breakthrough. No matter how things may look today, don't give in. Don't give up. Keep the faith. Your walls of Jericho are coming down.

Michele L. Smith

Today's Reflection:

Today's Prayer:

No Excuse Sunday

To make it possible for everyone to attend church next Sunday, we are going to have a special *"No Excuse Sunday."* Cots will be placed in the foyer for those who say, *'Sunday is my only day to sleep in.'* There will be a special section with lounge chairs for those who feel the pews are too hard. Eye drops will be available for those with tired eyes from watching T.V. late Saturday night. We will have steel helmets for those who say, *'The roof would cave in if I ever came to church.'* Blankets will be furnished for those who think the church is too cold and fans for those who say it is too hot. Score cards will be available for those who wish to list the hypocrites present. Relatives and friends will be in attendance for those who can't go to church and cook dinner too. We will distribute *'Stamp Out Stewardship'* buttons for those who feel that the church is always asking for money. One section will be devoted to trees and grass for those who like to see God in nature. Doctors and nurses will be in attendance for those who plan to be sick on Sunday. The sanctuary will be decorated with both Christmas poinsettias and Easter lilies for those who have never seen church without them. We will provide hearing aids for those who can't hear the preacher and cotton for those who say he is too loud!

See you Sunday!

"We are all here for some special reason. Stop being a prisoner to your past and become the architect of your future." Robin S.

Day 22 - Perfect Peace

This Day in History: Nobel peace prize awarded to Ralph J Bunche (1st black winner), September 22, 1950.

Today's Verse: *Peace I leave with you; my peace I give you. I do not give to you as the world gives. Do not let your hearts be troubled and do not be afraid.* **John 14:27**

Once upon a time a psychology professor walked around on a stage while teaching stress management principles to an auditorium filled with students. As she raised a glass of water, everyone expected they'd be asked the typical *"glass half empty or glass half full"* question. Instead, with a smile on her face, the professor asked, *"How heavy is this glass of water I'm holding?"*

Students shouted out answers ranging from eight ounces to a couple pounds.

She replied, *"From my perspective, the absolute weight of this glass doesn't matter. It all depends on how long I hold it. If I hold it for a minute or two, it's fairly light. If I hold it for an hour straight, its weight might make my arm ache a little. If I hold it for a day straight, my arm will likely cramp up and feel completely numb and paralyzed, forcing me to drop the glass to the floor. In each case, the weight of the glass doesn't change, but the longer I hold it, the heavier it feels to me."*

As the class shook their heads in agreement, she continued, *"Your stresses and worries in life are very much like this glass of water. Think about them for a while and nothing happens. Think about them a bit longer and you begin to ache a little. Think about them all day long, and you will feel completely numb and paralyzed – incapable of doing anything else until you drop them."*

Jesus tells us in John 14:27 that He give us peace. That our hearts need not be troubled, nor should we be afraid. We have to remember to let go of those things that stress and worry us. At the end of each day before you go to sleep, be sure to lay all your burdens before the Lord. Do not take them with you to sleep. Doing so will cause you to carry them into the next day.

It's important to remember to let go of your stresses and worries. No matter what happens during the day, as early in the evening as you can, put all your burdens down. Don't carry your glass into the next day. Put your glass down and Rest in His Perfect Peace.

Today's Reflection:

Today's Prayer:

Day 23 - Watch, Fight and Pray

Today's Verse: *I will therefore that men pray everywhere, lifting up holy hands, without wrath and doubting.* **I Timothy 2:8**

Joe Kennedy, a high school football coach and 20-year veteran of the U.S. Marine Corps is under investigation for praying with his players. Kennedy has been praying after games for nearly a decade, but he has never asked the kids to join him. They do so voluntarily. He's been warned that he could potentially lose his job. Supporters have posted pictures on social media in hopes of saving his job.

Are you aware that something dominates your every day? For some it's baby mama drama. For some it may be a controlling supervisor. Others may be dominated by events in the news. Yet others by financial woes. Joe Kennedy's days of late are inundated with threats of unemployment because he allows prayer to dominate his life. He understands that prayer is part of God's plan for his life. He has made the choice to allow God's will dominate his day. Prayer is a weapon. Prayer changes things. When fear tries to dominate your day, pray God has not given me the spirit of fear, but of love, power and a sound mind. When confusion tries to wreak havoc in your day, pray that God's Word dominate your day. When trials try to dominate your day, let peace dominate your day. When a negative mind tries to dominate your day, let the Holy Spirit take over and dominate your day. Don't despair, let your petitions in prayer dominate your day.

Today's Reflection:

Today's Prayer:

Day 24 - Beautiful are the Feet

This Day in History: Mahatma Ghandi released from jail, February 24, 1924.

Today's Verse: *And how shall they preach, except they be sent? As it is written, How beautiful are the feet of them that preach the gospel of peace, and bring glad tidings of good things!* **Romans 10:15**

Boomerang is a 1992 American romantic comedy film directed by Reginald Hudlin. Eddie Murphy stars as Marcus Graham, a hotshot advertising executive who also happens to be an insatiable womanizer and male chauvinist in the 1992 romantic comedy Boomerang. In one of the movie scenes Murphy is seen obsessing over the appearance of women's feet. He was in no way interested in any woman whose feet were unattractive.

The irony is that so many of us get caught up in physical appearances, struggle with issues of low self-esteem or having a long list of requirements for attributes when looking for a partner. Women spend hours getting spa pedicures, searching for the right color nail polish and the perfect stiletto to show off her feet. My aunt told me growing up, *"No man wants a woman with rough hands or ugly feet."*

John Ruskin said, *"When a man is wrapped up in himself, he makes a pretty small package."*

We all are conditioned to be self-centered, to think of ourselves. Have you noticed the majority of people will write their own name when offered to try a new pen? While we have this tendency to be self-serving, it is true that more is always accomplished when no one cares who gets the credit. God has called us to serve. God doesn't make leaders. God makes servants and servants become leaders. The way to the throne room is through the servant's quarters. God says, *"He that is greatest among you shall be your servant."* Matthew 23:33. Giving of yourself is service of others guarantees your abundant reward. It's not your Stacey Adams or Jimmy Choo's that make your feet fly. It is your willingness to serve that make your feet, your persona beautiful.

Today's Reflection:

Today's Prayer:

Day 25 - Write the Vision

This Day in History: Telegraph message sent from St Louis to San Francisco, October 25, 1861; Postcards first used in the United States, October 25, 1870.

Today's Verse: *And the Lord answered me, and said, Write the vision, and make it plain upon tables, that he may run that readeth it. For the vision is yet for an appointed time, but at the end it shall speak, and not lie: though it tarry, wait for it; because it will surely come, it will not tarry.* **Habakkuk 2:2-3**

Once up on a time there lived three fish in a pond. One was named *"Plan Ahead"*, another was *"Think Fast"*, and the third was named *"Wait and See"*. One day they heard a fisherman say that he was going to cast his net in their pond the next day.

Plan Ahead said, *"I'm swimming down the river tonight!"* and so he did.

Think Fast said, *"I'm sure I'll come up with a plan."*

Wait and See lazily said, *"I just can't think about it now!"*

When the fisherman cast his nets, Plan Ahead was long gone. But *"Think Fast"* and *"Wait and See"* were caught! *"Think Fast"* quickly rolled his belly up and pretended to be dead. *"Oh, this fish is no good!"* said the fisherman, and threw him safely back into the water. But, Wait and See ended up in the fish market.

That is why they say, *"In times of danger, when the net is cast, plan ahead or plan to think fast!"*

Regret looks back; worry looks around; faith looks up. Everyone should have vision in their life. Having a vision helps to plan ahead to avoid the danger like the fish *"Plan Ahead"*. Nothing great is created instantly. Ninety percent of success is starting and showing up. You begin with writing the vision. Dare to begin. You won't know you can do it until you try. People are like trees, we must grow or we wither. Standing still is not an option. You must begin to win.

Today's Reflection:

Today's Prayer:

Blessings and Gratitude

Trust in the LORD with all thine heart; and lean not unto thine own understanding. **Proverbs 3:5**

Michele L. Smith

"Very often a change of self is needed more than a change of scene."
A.C. Benson

Day 26 - Know, Grow and Go

This Day in History: First free kindergarten in the U.S. started by Susan Blow in Carondelet, a suburb of St. Louis, Missouri, August 26, 1873.

Today's Verse: *An intelligent heart acquires knowledge, and the ear of the wise seeks knowledge.* **Proverbs 18:15 (ESV)**

Once a fox was roaming around in the dark. Unfortunately, he fell into a well. He tried his level best to come out but all in vain. So, he had no other alternative but to remain there till the next morning. The next day, a goat came that way. She peeped into the well and saw the fox there. The goat asked *"what are you doing there, Mr. Fox?"*

The sly fox replied, *"I came here to drink water. It is the best I have ever tasted. Come and see for yourself."* Without thinking even for a while, the goat jumped into the well, quenched her thirst and looked for a way to get out. But just like the fox, she also found herself helpless to come out.

Then the fox said, *"I have an idea. You stand on your hind legs. I'll climb on your head and get out. Then I shall help you come out too."* The goat was innocent enough to understand the shrewdness of the fox and did as the fox said and helped him get out of the well.

While walking away, the fox said, *"Had you been intelligent enough, you would never have got in without seeing how to get out."*

Looking back over your life, can you recall some well experiences? Those times when you took a leap without checking out the surroundings or considering the possibilities? Look before you leap. Do not just blindly walk in to anything without thinking. You are equipped with all that you need to succeed. Failing to plan is planning to fail. Look before you leap.

Today's Reflection:

Today's Prayer:

Day 27 - The Good Fight

Today's Verse: *Fight the good of faith, lay hold on eternal life, whereunto thou art also called, and hast professed a good profession before many witnesses.* **I Timothy 6:12**

One of my favorite stories from the Bible is found in the book of Esther. Esther was a Jew, taken as the wife of Ahasuerus, the king of the Persians and Medes. Esther was chosen after reportedly a period of at least a year-long of training and preparation to be presented to the king.

There was a minister in the king's court named Haman who devised an evil plot to eliminate the Jews. Mordecai, Esther's uncle, learned of the plot and told Esther she had to talk to the king about Haman's plan. Though Esther was the queen, their relationship was not like that of husbands and wives today. She couldn't just go to the king whenever she pleased. She needed to request an audience of the king just like anyone else would. To enter the king's presence without an invitation could get Esther killed.

Mordecai advised Esther that she was brought to the position she had *"for such a time as this."* (Esther 4:14) She fasted and prayed. Esther decided she would stand up for her people even if it meant death. She trusted God to order her steps in revealing the Haman's plot against her people to the king.

By faith, Esther revealed Haman's plan. The king listened and Esther's heritage as a child of God's people, and the Jews were saved from the evil intended for them. By faith, we must stand in the face of adversity today. By faith, we must boldly expose the wicked devices of the enemy. By faith, we must profess the blessings of God over ourselves, our families, our neighborhoods, communities and our churches. By faith, we enter the presence of the King of Kings, God our Father to receive our royal inheritance as sons and daughter of the Most High.

Today's Reflection:

Today's Prayer:

Day 28 - Great Catch

This Day in History: United States Supreme Court (8-0) overturns draft evasion conviction of Muhammad Ali, June 28, 1971.

Today's Verse: *Two are better than one; because they have a good reward for their labour. For if they fall, the one will lift up his fellow: but woe to him that is alone when he falleth; for he hath not another to help him up. Again, if two lie together, then they have heat: but how can one be warm alone? And if one prevail against him, two shall withstand him; and a threefold cord is not quickly broken.* **Ecclesiastes 4:9-12**

The sport of baseball took on a personal meaning to me in the early 1980's when I met a young man who played on the team at Long Beach City College. He was good in the outfield, but everyone loved watching his efforts to advance the offense by 'stealing bases.' Stealing in the game of baseball requires intense concentration, skill and calculated speed. I can still hear the thunderous roar of applause whenever he was successful at stealing a base. Then there were the negative shouts if he got caught.

Sometimes the hardest part about being a great catch is accepting that not everyone's hands are strong enough to hold you. You must know that their inability to hold you doesn't make you any less valuable. Everyone cannot have a seat in the stadium of your life. Everyone is not going to root for you to reach all the bases. Everyone is not capable of applauding your home runs. You must learn to discern, to dig your cleats in and run when the opportunity is there for you to advance. Surround yourself with those who are amazing individual players, but will take one for the team, if needed. Learn how to toot your own horn. Celebrate your personal victories and Live Your Life Royally.

Today's Reflection:

Today's Prayer:

Work In Progress

From the moment of conception,
Until we take our first breath
From the moment of our birth,
Until the time of our death
We're taught what to do and what not to
Yet of all the lessons we learn in life
There's one that suits us best
And that is to remember
That we are merely a Work In Progress!
From the moment of salvation,
From the hour of baptism
We seek the solace of the Lord,
 In the comfort that He's risen
Risen high above the earth all power in His hands
Watching daily as we grow
Learning the laws of the land
And in our Christian walk with God
Learning love and faithfulness
Daily we must remember that we are merely a Work In Progress!
When someone makes you angry
And another makes you cry
When things are not going quite your way
And you don't understand why
When the car breaks down and the bills are due
When you feel pretty lost
And aren't sure of what to do
Spend some time remembering His suffering
And all Jesus gave for you
Remember His sacrifice
And daily renewed forgiveness
Remember that we are merely a Work In Progress!
Beings that once were lost
And now have life renewed
Remember that He cares today

The same as when He died for you
When you feel tired and don't want to go on
Remember for you He carried the cross
And wore the crown of thorns
When you are sad and all worn out
When your life's a mess and you're full of doubt
Remember you deserve to have nothing but the best
Remember that this life
Is merely a Work In Progress!
Don't cast your eyes down on others
You must instead love your sisters and brothers
Don't let your mind be a playground for Satan
Don't spend your time being jealous and hatin'
For you must look deep within
And deal with the mess of your own sin
You must die to self and selfishness,
For you are merely a Work In Progress!
Your life is like a mold of clay
Molded by the potter's hands
Your shape is formed and strengthened
Each time you take a stand
A stand to live a Godly life
In spite of all the trials and strife
A stand to be a Christian child,
Helping someone else feel worthwhile
Your journey here is a simple one
And you must stay the course and run
Run the race He made for you,
Saving others and giving more
More of the love He gives to you,
Pass along His grace and awesome goodness
Never forget you are God's Work In Progress!

Michele L. Smith

"Chase your passion like it's the last bus of the night."
Sheila P. Spencer

Day 29 - Dare to Dream Big

This Day in History: "Gone with the Wind," wins 8 Oscars at the 12th Academy Awards; Hattie McDaniel becomes 1st black woman to win an Oscar, February 29, 1940.

Today's Verse: *But Joseph dreamed still another dream, and told it to his brothers [as well]. He said, "See here, I have again dreamed a dream, and lo, [this time I saw] eleven stars and the sun and the moon bowed down [in respect] to me!"* **Genesis 37:9 (AMP)**

As a senior, a young man was asked to write a paper about what he wanted to be and do when he grew up. That night he wrote a seven-page paper describing his goal of someday owning a horse ranch. He detailed his dream, drew a diagram of a 200-acre ranch, the stables, the track and a 4,000-square foot house. He poured his heart into the project and handed it in to his teacher.

Two days later he received his paper back with a large red F with a note that read, *"See me after class.'"*

The boy went to see the teacher after class and asked, *"Why did I receive an F?'"* The teacher said, *"This is an unrealistic dream for a young boy like you. You have no money, no resources and you come from a poor family. A project like this requires a lot of money. There's no way you could ever do it."* Then the teacher added, *"If you will rewrite this paper with a more realistic goal, I will reconsider your grade."*

After giving careful consideration, the boy asked his father what he should do. His father said, *"`Look, son, you have to make up* *your own mind on this. However, I think it is a very important decision for you.*"

A week later, after much contemplation, the boy turned in the same paper, making no changes at all. He stated, *"You can keep the F and I'll keep my dream."*

Years later the boy realized his dream and that same teacher brought 30 kids to his ranch for a week. As he was leaving the teacher told the young man, *"When I was your teacher, I was something of a dream stealer. During those years I stole a lot of kids' dreams. Fortunately you had enough gumption not to give up on yours.'*"

Don't let anyone crush or steal your dreams. When what you see is so big there's no way you can pay for it, there's no way you can accomplish it on your own, you don't see any way possible for it to come to pass that's when you know it's God. Far too often we delay the manifestation of our dreams coming true by thinking that God needs our help. Or that because we are not in position to make it happen right now that God can't do it either. The earth is the Lord's and the fullness thereof. There is nothing too big or too hard for God. As his child, there is nothing too big or too hard for you either. Dare to Dream. Dare to Dream Big. Keep climbing until all your Dreams Come True.

Today's Reflection:

Today's Prayer:

Day 30 - Weapons of Warfare

This Day in History: President Bill Clinton signs Brady Gun Control Bill, November 30, 1993.

Today's Verse: *Wherefore take unto you the whole armor of God, that ye may be able to withstand in the evil day, and having done all, to stand.* **Ephesians 6:13**

Soldiers in each branch of the military undergo rigorous training and extensive preparation so that they are ready on a moment's notice to man the front line in defense of our country. Upon checking in to boot camp each soldier is provided standard issue uniforms, shoes and are subjected to a battery of medical tests and other exams to ensure they are fit and adequately dressed for the call of duty. As soldiers in the army of the Lord, we are provided the armor of God. Stand therefore, having your loins girt about with truth, and having on the breastplate of righteousness; And your feet shod with the preparation of the gospel of peace; Above all, taking the shield of faith, wherewith ye shall be able to quench all the fiery darts of the wicked. And take the helmet of salvation, and the sword of the Spirit, which is the word of God: Praying always with all prayer and supplication in the Spirit, and watching thereunto with all perseverance and supplication for all saints; Ephesians 3:14-18.

Employees in some companies are required to wear the company uniform when working. Showing up out of uniform could result in reprimand, time off without pay or even loss of your job. Leaving home without your armor makes you a target for negativity and attack. Don't leave home without putting your armor on. You don't want to be out in public half-dressed. Praying as you dress in the natural and in the spirit is your insurance. Prayer is the pin code to your emergency roadside assistance. Clothing yourself in the whole armor of God will make you the best dressed person wherever you go. Be it work, ministry or play, use the weapons of warfare to dominate your day.

Michele L. Smith

Today's Reflection:

Today's Prayer:

Blessings and Gratitude

If there be therefore any consolation in Christ, if any comfort of love, if any fellowship of the Spirit, if any bowels and mercies, Fulfil ye my joy, that ye be likeminded, having the same love, being of one accord, of one mind. **Philippians 2:1-2**

Michele L. Smith

"He who rejects change is the architect of decay. The only human institution which rejects progress is the cemetery." Harold Wilson

Thirty Days Hath September

Thirty days hath September,
April, June and November;
February has twenty eight alone
All the rest have thirty-one
Except in Leap Year, that's the time
When February's Days are twenty-nine

Bonus Day 1 - Believe

This Day in History: George Foreman KOs Jose "King" Roman in 1 for heavyweight boxing title, September 1, 1973.

Today's Verse: *And Jesus said unto them, Because of your unbelief: for verily I say unto you, If ye have faith as a grain of mustard seed, ye shall say unto this mountain, Remove hence to yonder place; and it shall remove; and nothing shall be impossible unto you.* **Matthew 17:20**

A man just got married and was returning home with his wife. They were crossing a lake in a boat, when suddenly a great storm arose. The man was a warrior, but the woman became very much afraid because it seemed almost hopeless: The boat was small and the storm was really huge, and any moment they were going to be drowned. But the man sat silently, calm and quiet, as if nothing was happening.

The woman was trembling and she said, *"Are you not afraid? This may be our last moment of life! Only some miracle can save us; otherwise death is certain. Are you mad or something? Are you a stone or something?"*

The man laughed and took the sword out of its sheath. The woman was even more puzzled: What he was doing? Then he brought the naked sword close to the woman's neck, so close that just a small gap was there, it was almost touching her neck. He said, *"Are you afraid?"*

She started to laugh and said, *"Why should I be afraid? I know you love me."* He put the sword back and said, *"I know God Loves me, and the storm is in His hands. Whatever happens, it's going to be good. If we survive, good; if we don't survive, good, because everything is in His hands."*

When the storms in your life arise, do you have faith to believe? God says this day: Dare to BELIEVE in You...Not because everything is great, but because even at your weakest moment, you are Powerful, Passionate and full of Purpose. BELIEVE in Faith...Not because you can see the whole staircase, but because you are taking the first step. BELIEVE in Love...Not because it's always perfect, but because Love Conquers All. BELIEVE in God like you believe in the sunrise. Not because you can see it, but because you can See ALL that it touches. BELIEVE and Live Your Life Royally!

Today's Reflection:

Today's Prayer:

Bonus Day 2 - Slow Your Role

This Day in History: President Nixon signs national speed limit into law, January 2, 1974.

Today's Verse: *And let us not be weary in well doing: for in due season we shall reap, if we faint not.* **Galatians 6:9**

One of the first characters of the Bible I recall learning about is Job. I often heard people talk about the 'patience of Job.' How he lost everything but never cursed God.

To prove Job's faithfulness to the Lord, God allowed the devil to destroy everything Job owned (Job 1). Job was a wealthy man. He lost his servants, crops and property, cattle and servants. Most devastating was likely when Job lost his children. His friends tried to get in his ear, dipping all in the kool-aid trying to find out what Job had done. But, Job admitted no wrong-doing, nor did he blame God. He trusted that God had a plan and he would be patient and wait for God to reveal it to him. In the end God restored to Job twice as much as he had in the beginning (Job 42:10).

God has called each of us and we need to continue in patience and faith even when it looks as though there's no progress. Even Jesus taught His disciples until the moment of His death. Follow the examples of Job and Jesus. You might lose some stuff (material possessions). Some people may fall away. The length of the storm may seem extensive, but let patience have her perfect work and God will give you double for your trouble just as He did Job.

Michele L. Smith

Today's Reflection:

Today's Prayer:

Bonus Day 3 - Stay the Course

This Day in History: Calvin Smith of U.S. becomes fastest man alive (9.93 for 100m), July 3, 1983.

Today's Verse: *Where there is no vision, the people perish: but he that keepeth the law, happy is he.* **Proverbs 29:18**

Life can be unpredictable. Some days the path gets a lil bumpy. You may come across some potholes or cracks in the road. The main thing is to keep the main thing the main thing and not allow the pitfalls to suck you into a black hole of despair. When you've done all you can do, just stand and stay on the path. You may get tired, but don't grow weary. God said, How beautiful are the feet of them that preach the gospel of peace, and bring glad tidings of good things! So don't stop walking. Stay the course. Somebody is waiting for you to arrive. You are the courier of someone's blessing. You may be carrying someone's healing, deliverance or salvation. You may even have all three. Either way, they won't get what they need if you don't show up. The road you're traveling may seem uphill, there may be tests of your courage and will. But no matter how hard things seem, you must not quit. For every test has a time limit, every trial an expiration date. Be assured and encouraged for God is with you always and He is never late. Stay the course and you will cross the finish line right on time. Stay the course – Victory is yours in Christ Jesus.

Michele L. Smith

Today's Reflection:

Today's Prayer:

Bonus Day 4 - Daily Reminders

This Day in History: "Dreamgirls" closes at Imperial Theater NYC after 1522 performances, August 4, 1985.

Today's Verse: *And thou shalt love the LORD thy God with all thine heart, and with all they soul, and with all thy might.* **Deuteronomy 6:5**

God should be first and foremost in our lives. When He is you're A#1 it doesn't matter what happens, you are assured that everything is working for your good. Today's Daily Reminders are designed to help you in having your best day every day. Putting on a Smile each day is scientifically proven to bring positive results. Without faith nothing is possible. With faith all things are possible. You have to Believe in something or you will Fall for anything. What's Love got to do with it, you ask? Everything! It's ALL about Love. For God so Loved that He Gave. It's because of love that we live, move and have our being. Love is the most powerful force. Look around and you'll see how powerful the power of love can be. And finally, there's Prayer. Many underestimate the impact of prayer. Don't just pray when you're in a crisis. Make prayer a part of your every day and watch the negativity dissolve away.

Michele L. Smith

Today's Reflection:

Today's Prayer:

116

Bonuſ Day 5 - Ways to Love

Today's Verse: *For God so loved the world, that he gave his only begotten Son, that whosoever believeth in him should not perish, but have everlasting life.* **John 3:16**

Love is the first command given by God and is not something we should take lightly. Following are ten verses on how to love. When you allow Love to Abide you are certain to Live Your Life Royally.

*Listen without interrupting: Through desire a man, having separated himself, seeketh and intermeddleth with all wisdom. A fool hath no delight in understanding, but that his heart may discover itself. When the wicked cometh, then cometh also contempt, and with ignominy reproach. The words of a man's mouth are as deep waters, and the wellspring of wisdom as a flowing brook. Proverbs 18

*Speak without accusing: Wherefore, my beloved brethren, let every man be swift to hear, slow to speak, slow to wrath: James 1:19

*Give without sparing: He coveteth greedily all the day long: but the righteous giveth and spareth not. Proverbs 21:26

*Honor without fail: Marriage is honourable in all, and the bed undefiled: but whoremongers and adulterers God will judge. Hebrews 13:4

*Answer without arguing: Better is a dry morsel, and

Quietness therewith, than an house full of sacrifices with strife. Proverbs 17:1

*Share without pretending: But speaking the truth in love, may grow up into him in all things, which is the head, even Christ: Ephesians 4:15

*Enjoy without complaint: Do all things without murmurings and disputings: Philippians 2:14

*Trust without wavering: Every man's work shall be made manifest: for the day shall declare it, because it shall be revealed by fire; and the fire shall try every man's work of what sort it is. I Corinthians 3:13

*Promise without forgetting: Hope deferred maketh the heart sick: but when the desire cometh, it is a tree of life. Proverbs 13:12

Today's Reflection:

Today's Prayer:

Bonus Day 6 - The Choice is Yours

Today's Verse: *See then that ye walk circumspectly, not as fools, but as wise, Redeeming the time, because the days are evil. Wherefore be ye not unwise, but understanding what the will of the Lord is.* **Ephesians 5:15-17**

One of my Facebook friends and sister in the Lord shares Would You Rather questions on her timeline that are funny and often thought provoking when you ponder the possibilities. Example: Would you rather...have your ears where your eyebrows are – OR – have your nose where your belly button is? Would you rather...Be 20 feet off the ground, climbing a tree, when you realize it's covered with really sticky sap – OR – covered with millions of tiny ants?

Reading these brings to mind a quote I read some time ago about believing in God that stuck with me like glue on a postage stamp: I would rather live my life as though there is a God and die to find out there isn't, than to live my life as though there isn't and die to find out there is. Would you rather? I've made my choice. What about you?

We are living in a time when those who don't believe, and some who do, choose to sugar coat or ignore the Word of God in order to fit their own agenda. This is becoming more of a standard than a minority. It's time for the Body of Christ to disembark from the Woe is Me train and begin to Stand for Truth. This does not mean retaliate in violence or act out in hate. It does not mean that we demean or negate the beliefs of others. Simply put, it means we walk in God's Love. Forgive those who despitefully use you. Repent for the wrong you have done. Repent on behalf of those who know not what they do.

Many today are living in an identity crisis and are so lost in deception they don't even know it. And behold, I come quickly: and my reward is with me, to give every man according as his work shall be. I am Alpha and Omega, the beginning of the end, the first and the last. Blessed are they that do his commandments, that they might have right to the tree of life, and may enter in through the gates into the city. For without are dogs, and sorcerers, and whoremongers, and murderers, and idolaters, and whosoever loveth and maketh a lie. I Jesus have sent mine angel to testify unto you these things in the churches. I am the root and offspring of David, and the bright and morning star. And the spirit and the bride say, Come. And let him that heareth say, Come. And let him that is athirst come. And whosoever will, let him take the water of life freely. Revelation 22:12-17.

God is asking today…Would you rather? The Choice is yours. God is saying, "Ready or not here I come. How will I find you?" Will He be able to identify you when He comes? Will you be ready to Live Your Life Eternally?

Michele L. Smith

Today's Reflection:

Today's Prayer:

Blessings and Gratitude

Today's Verse: *For I know the thoughts that I think toward you, saith the Lord, thoughts of peace, and not of evil, to give you an expected end.* **Jeremiah 29:11**

Michele L. Smith

"When you are through changing, you are through." Bruce Barton

Bible Reading Plan

Reading the referenced passage each day, you will read the entire Bible in one year. Start reading today, there is no better time than the present. Schedule a specific time each day for your personal reading. Pray when you begin. Ask the Holy Spirit for wisdom and understanding. Keep track of your reading and enjoy your journey through the Word of God.

Date	Passage	Completed
1	Genesis 1-4	
2	Genesis 5-8	
3	Genesis 9-12	
4	Genesis 13-17	
5	Genesis 18-20	
6	Genesis 21-23	
7	Genesis 24-25	
8	Genesis 26-28	
9	Genesis 29-31	
10	Genesis 32-35	
11	Genesis 36-38	
12	Genesis 39-41	
13	Genesis 42-43	
14	Genesis 44-46	

15	Genesis 47-50	
16	Exodus 1-4	
17	Exodus 5-7	
18	Exodus 8-10	
19	Exodus 11-13	
20	Exodus 14-16	
21	Exodus 17-20	
22	Exodus 21-23	
23	Exodus 24-27	
24	Exodus 28-30	
25	Exodus 31-34	
26	Exodus 35-37	
27	Exodus 38-40	
28	Leviticus 1-4	
29	Leviticus 5-7	
30	Leviticus 8-10	
31	Leviticus 11-13	
32	Leviticus 14-15	
33	Leviticus 16-18	
34	Leviticus 19-21	
35	Leviticus 22-23	
36	Leviticus 24-25	
37	Leviticus 26-27	

38	Numbers 1-2	
39	Numbers 3-4	
40	Numbers 5-6	
41	Numbers 7	
42	Numbers 8-10	
43	Numbers 11-13	
44	Numbers 14-15	
45	Numbers 16-18	
46	Numbers 19-21	
47	Numbers 22-24	
48	Numbers 25-26	
49	Numbers 27-29	
50	Numbers 30-32	
51	Numbers 33-36	
52	Deuteronomy 1-2	
53	Deuteronomy 3-4	
54	Deuteronomy 5-8	
55	Deuteronomy 9-11	
56	Deuteronomy 12-15	
57	Deuteronomy16-19	
58	Deuteronomy 20-22	
59	Deuteronomy 23-25	
60	Deuteronomy 26-27	

61	Deuteronomy 28-29	
62	Deuteronomy 30-32	
63	Deuteronomy 33-34	
64	Joshua 1-4	
65	Joshua 5-7	
66	Joshua 8-10	
67	Joshua 11-13	
68	Joshua 14-17	
69	Joshua 18-20	
70	Joshua 21-22	
71	Joshua 23-24	
72	Judges 1-3	
73	Judges 4-5	
74	Judges 6-8	
75	Judges 9-10	
76	Judges 11-13	
77	Judges 14-16	
78	Judges 17-19	
79	Judges 20-21	
80	Ruth 1-4	
81	I Samuel 1-3	
82	I Samuel 4-7	
83	I Samuel 8-12	

84	I Samuel 13-14	
85	I Samuel 15-16	
86	I Samuel 17-18	
87	I Samuel19-21	
88	I Samuel 22-24	
89	I Samuel 25-27	
90	I Samuel 28-31	
91	II Samuel 1-3	
92	II Samuel 4-7	
93	II Samuel 8-11	
94	II Samuel 12-13	
95	II Samuel 14-16	
96	II Samuel 17-19	
97	II Samuel 20-22	
98	II Samuel 23-24	
99	I Kings 1-2	
100	I Kings 3-5	
101	I Kings 6-7	
102	I Kings 8-9	
103	I Kings 10-12	
104	I Kings 13-15	
105	I Kings 16-18	
106	I Kings 19-20	

107	I Kings 21-22	
108	II Kings 1-3	
109	II Kings 4-5	
110	II Kings 6-8	
111	II Kings9-10	
112	II Kings 11-13	
113	II Kings 14-16	
114	II Kings 17-18	
115	II Kings 19-21	
116	II Kings 22-23	
117	II Kings 24-25	
118	I Chronicles 1-2	
119	I Chronicles 3-4	
120	I Chronicles 5-6	
121	I Chronicles 7-9	
122	I Chronicles 10-12	
123	I Chronicles 13-16	
124	I Chronicles 17-19	
125	I Chronicles 20-23	
126	I Chronicles 24-26	
127	I Chronicle 27-29	
128	II Chronicles 1-4	
129	II Chronicles 5-7	

130	II Chronicles 8-11	
131	II Chronicles 12-16	
132	II Chronicles 17-20	
133	II Chronicles 21-24	
134	II Chronicles 25-28	
135	II Chronicles 29-31	
136	II Chronicles 32-34	
137	II Chronicles 35-36	
138	Ezra 1-4	
139	Ezra 5-7	
140	Ezra 8-10	
141	Nehemiah 1-3	
142	Nehemiah 4-7	
143	Nehemiah 8-10	
144	Nehemiah 11-13	
145	Esther 1-5	
146	Esther 6-10	
147	Job 1-4	
148	Job 5-8	
149	Job 9-12	
150	Job 13-16	
151	Job 17-20	
152	Job 21-24	

153	Job 25-30	
154	Job 31-34	
155	Job 35-38	
156	Jo 39-42	
157	Psalms 1-8	
158	Psalms 9-17	
159	Psalms 18-21	
160	Psalms 22-27	
161	Psalms 28-33	
162	Psalms 34-37	
163	Psalms 38-42	
164	Psalms 43-49	
165	Psalms 50-55	
166	Psalms 56-61	
167	Psalms 62-68	
168	Psalms 69-72	
169	Psalms 73-77	
170	Psalms 78-80	
171	Psalms 81-88	
172	Psalms 89-94	
173	Psalms 95-103	
174	Psalms 104-106	
175	Psalms 107-111	

176	Psalms 112-118	
177	Psalms 119	
178	Psalms 120-133	
179	Psalms 134-140	
180	Psalms 141-150	
181	Proverbs 1-3	
182	Proverbs 4-7	
183	Proverbs 8-11	
184	Proverbs 12-14	
185	Proverbs 15-17	
186	Proverbs 18-20	
187	Proverbs 21-23	
188	Proverbs 24-26	
189	Proverbs 27-29	
190	Proverbs 30-31	
191	Ecclesiastes 1-4	
192	Ecclesiastes 5-8	
193	Ecclesiastes 9-12	
194	Song of Solomon 1-4	
195	Song of Solomon 5-8	
196	Isaiah 1-3	
197	Isaiah 4-8	
198	Isaiah 9-11	

199	Isaiah 12-14	
200	Isaiah 15-19	
201	Isaiah 20-24	
202	Isaiah 25-28	
203	Isaiah 29-31	
204	Isaiah 32-34	
205	Isaiah 35-37	
206	Isaiah 38-40	
207	Isaiah 41-43	
208	Isaiah 44-46	
209	Isaiah 47-49	
210	Isaiah 50-52	
211	Isaiah 53-56	
212	Isaiah 57-59	
213	Isaiah 60-63	
214	Isaiah 64-66	
215	Jeremiah 1-3	
216	Jeremiah 4-5	
217	Jeremiah 6-8	
218	Jeremiah 9-11	
219	Jeremiah 12-14	
220	Jeremiah 15-17	
221	Jeremiah 18-21	

222	Jeremiah 22-24	
223	Jeremiah 25-27	
224	Jeremiah 28-30	
225	Jeremiah 31-32	
226	Jeremiah 33-36	
227	Jeremiah 37-39	
228	Jeremiah 40-43	
229	Jeremiah 44-46	
230	Jeremiah 47-48	
231	Jeremiah 49	
232	Jeremiah 50	
233	Jeremiah 51-52	
234	Lamentations 1-2	
235	Lamentations 3-5	
236	Ezekiel 1-4	
237	Ezekiel 5-8	
238	Ezekiel 9-12	
239	Ezekiel 13-15	
240	Ezekiel 16-17	
241	Ezekiel 18-20	
242	Ezekiel 21-22	
243	Ezekiel 23-24	
244	Ezekiel 25-27	

245	28-30	
246	31-32	
247	33-35	
248	36-38	
249	39-40	
250	41-43	
251	44-46	
252	47-48	
253	Daniel 1-3	
254	4-5	
255	6-8	
256	9-12	
257	Hosea 1-4	
258	Hosea 5-9	
259	Hosea 10-14	
260	Joel 1-3	
261	Amos 1-4	
262	Amos 5-9	
263	Obadiah 1	
264	Jonah 1-4	
265	Micah 1-4	
266	Micah 5-7	
267	Nahum 1-3	

268	Habakkuk 1-3	
269	Zephaniah 1-3	
270	Haggai 1-2	
271	Zechariah 1-5	
272	6-10	
273	11-14	
274	Malachi 1-4	
275	Matthew 1-4	
276	5-6	
277	7-9	
278	10-11	
279	12-13	
280	14-17	
281	18-20	
282	21-22	
283	23-24	
284	25-26	
285	27-28	
286	Mark 1-3	
287	4-5	
288	6-7	
289	8-9	
290	10-11	

291	12-13	
292	14	
293	15-16	
294	Luke 1-2	
295	3-4	
296	5-6	
297	7-8	
298	9-10	
299	11-12	
300	13-15	
301	16-18	
302	19-20	
303	21-22	
304	23-24	
305	John 1-2	
306	3-4	
307	5-6	
308	7-8	
309	9-10	
310	11-12	
311	13-15	
312	16-17	
313	John 18-19	

314	John 20-21	
315	Acts 1-3	
316	Acts 4-5	
317	Acts 6-7	
318	Acts 8-9	
319	Acts 10-11	
320	Acts 12-13	
321	Acts 14-15	
322	Acts 16-17	
323	Acts 18-19	
324	Acts 20-21	
325	Acts 22-23	
326	Acts 24-26	
327	Acts 27-28	
328	Romans 1-3	
329	Romans 4-7	
330	Romans 8-10	
331	Romans 11-14	
332	Romans 15-16	
333	I Corinthians 1-4	
334	I Corinthians 5-9	
335	I Corinthians 10-13	
336	I Corinthians 14-16	

337	II Corinthians 1-4	
338	II Corinthians 5-9	
339	II Corinthians 10-13	
340	Galatians 1-3	
341	Galatians 4-6	
342	Ephesians 1-3	
343	Ephesians 4-6	
344	Philippians 1-4	
345	Colossians 1-4	
346	I Thessalonians 1-5	
347	II Thessalonians 1-3	
348	I Timothy 1-6	
349	II Timothy 1-4	
350	Philemon 1; Titus 1-3	
351	Hebrews 1-4	
352	Hebrews 5-8	
353	Hebrews 9-10	
354	Hebrews 11-13	
355	James 1-5	
356	I Peter 1-5; 2 Peter 1-3	
357	I John 1-5	
358	2 John 1; 3 John 1; Jude 1	
359	Revelation 1-3	

360	Revelation 4-7	
361	Revelation 8-11	
362	Revelation 12-14	
363	Revelation 15-17	
364	Revelation 18-19	
365	Revelation 20-22	

I Am Affirmations

"And you will know the truth, and the truth will make you free." John 8:32. There are a great many Biblical truths that reveal who God made you to be. People say, *"You are what you eat."* Truth is, you are what you speak. As a man thinketh, so is he. Following are some I AM Affirmations. This is not meant to be a total list of all the Bible says that you are. Read them daily. Confess them out loud. Add to the list or create your own. Speak your I Am into existence. Speak those things that be not as though they were. Manifest Your I Am to Live Your Life Royally.

I Am a Believer (2 Corinthians 4:4).

I Am fearfully and wonderfully made (Psalm 139:14).

I Am in His perfect peace (Isaiah 26:3).

I Am more than a conqueror (Romans 8:37).

I Am a New Creation (2 Corinthians 5:17).

I Am able to do all things through Christ Jesus (Philippians 4:13).

I Am God's child (1 Peter 1:23).

I Am God's workmanship (Ephesians 2:10).

I Am a doer of the Word (James 1:22,25).

I Am a joint-heir with Christ (Romans 8:17).

Royal Words to Guide Your Day

I Am a royal priesthood, a holy nation (1 Peter 2:9).

I Am Holy and without blame (Ephesians 1:4; 1 Peter 1:16).

I Am the righteousness of God in Jesus Christ
(2 Corinthians 5:21).

I Am the temple of the Holy Spirit; (1 Corinthians 6:19).

I Am the head and not the tail; I am above only and not beneath
(Deuteronomy 28:13).

I Am the light of the world (Matthew 5:14).

I Am the salt of the earth (Matthew 5:13).

I Am His elect, (Romans 8:33; Colossians 3:12).

I Am forgiven (Ephesians 1:7).

I Am redeemed (Deuteronomy 28:15-68; Galatians 3:13).

I Am firmly rooted, built up, established in my faith
(Colossians 2:7).

I Am Healed by Jesus' stripes (Isaiah 53:5).

I Am loved (Romans 1:7; 1 Thessalonians 1:4).

I Am Victorious (Philippians 3:14).

I Am Fearless (2 Timothy 1:7).

References

www.brainyquote.com

www.history.com/this-day-in-history

www.christianity.com

www.livin3.com

www.boardofwisdom.com

www.biblegateway.com

About the Author

Michele "Princess Mimi" Smith

The devotions contained in this first volume of *Royal Words to Guide Your Day* are the result of Michele's life experience, her deep desire to encourage others and her faith in God. She has a servant's heart and has been pivotal in helping others change direction by virtue of loving, edifying and empowering them. Michele has pledged herself to work relentlessly serving inner-city and impoverished children, youth and young adults.

Michele has attended and served at El Shaddai Christian Church in Los Angeles, California since 2002 in the Ministry and Leadership Training Class. She is the owner of Royal Word Publications, a publishing and consulting company. She is also President of Precious Nuggets Communications, a non-profit corporation spearheaded to fund scholarships, school supplies and provide resources to impoverished and disadvantaged students across the United States.

Her writing has opened the door for her to express her love to a hurting world. She is dedicated to empowering and inspiring others.

Royal Words is a powerful read, straight from the soul of one woman whose Christian faith is near and dear to her heart. Michele's intense passion for writing is evident within the pages of this missive. She has penned numerous poems and recited them at various conferences and poetry readings. Her well-respected and faith-based writings have inspired many individuals to pursue their own respective calling. To learn more about Michele and her upcoming projects visit her website: www.royalwordpublications.com.

www.ingramcontent.com/pod-product-compliance
Lightning Source LLC
Chambersburg PA
CBHW052008090426
42741CB00008B/1601

* 9 7 8 0 6 9 2 5 2 0 8 7 1 *